The Ramen Budget:

How to Save Money by Cooking with Everyone's Favorite Staple

Ingrid DeWitt

The Ramen Budget: How to Save Money by Cooking with Everyone's Favorite Staple

All rights reserved. No part of this book may be reproduced in any form or by any electronic or mechanical means, without written permission of the author, except where permitted by law.

Text by Ingrid DeWitt

Cover design by Ingrid DeWitt. Credit for the cover photo goes to the-creative-exchange, whose excellent photography can be found on Unsplash.

Photos used under a Free to Use Unsplash License.

DeWitt, Ingrid.

The Ramen Budget: How to Save Money by Cooking with Everyone's Favorite Staple

Version 1.0 August 2019

Acknowledgements

Uncountable thanks and hugs to my team of loved ones for helping put this project together. In addition to beta-testing the recipes of this book, I owe Natalie, Kristen, Michael, and Sara tremendous thanks in letting me bring ramen-based dishes to our monthly get-togethers. I'm sure that by now they are ramened-out for a long time!

This book is for everyone who finds themselves needing to cut costs and corners during those tough times in life. Graduate and undergraduate students have a special place in my heart and are the inspiration and audience I kept in mind throughout putting together this guide.

Bon Appetit, and bon budget!

Table of Contents

The Mission and Origins of this Book
- The Cost of Eating
- But What if this Isn't Enough?
- The Origins of the Ramen Budget
- On the Limits of Individual Actions: A Disclaimer

The Math of The Ramen Budget

Price Breakdown

Ingredients and Costs
- Cutting Costs Further on Ingredients

The Recipes
- Breakfast
  - Scrambled eggs
  - Omelet
  - Ramen Crusted French Toast
  - Breakfast Scramble
  - Breakfast Veggie
  - Breakfast Burrito
  - Ramen Frittata
  - Bacon and Egg Ramen
- Soup-Based Dishes
  - Pork Noodle Soup
  - Chicken and Noodle Tomato Soup
  - Red Curry Carrot Soup
  - Ham Ramen Navy Beans
  - Potato Cheese Soup
  - Ramen Corn Chowder

- Broccoli Soup
- Hot Noodle Dishes
  - Sesame Chicken Noodle
  - Beef and Mushroom Sesame Noodles
  - Stir Fry Pork
  - Chicken Lo Mein
  - Spinach Ramen
  - Italian Cheese and Pepper Pasta
  - Teriyaki Meatballs and Ramen
- Pasta Salads
  - Strawberry Ramen Salad
  - Sesame Ramen Salad
  - Chicken Noodle Salad
  - Broccoli Noodle Salad
- International Fusion
  - Hoisin Pork Tenderloin
  - Ramen Latkes
  - Pad Thai
  - Peanut Thai Ramen
  - Ramen Katsu
  - Pho Ramen
  - Tom Kha Goong
  - Chimichanga
  - Noodle Pancakes
  - Tropical Ramen
  - Lettuce Wraps
- Fast Food Fusion
  - Ramen Tacos

- Sweet & Sour Ramen
- Cheesy Chili Ramen
- Ramen Poutine
- Ramen Pizza
- Ramen White Pizza

Desserts
- Ramen Brownies
- Ramen Krispies
- Strawberry Ramen Shortcake
- White Chocolate Ramen Bark
- Banana-Coconut Ramen Pudding
- Flan Ramen

Snacks
- Ramen Crunch Mix
- Sweet Ramen Crunch

The Mission and Origins of this Book

This book is about ramen. It is full of recipes to cook and eat ramen creatively, and is meant to expand culinary horizons using one of the most basic college food staples. You could use this book purely as a cookbook, referencing it when you want to try a new recipe or reference a meal you ate and enjoyed.

At the same time, this book is also much more than that. It is a roadmap and plan for people hoping to boost their saving or temporarily cut-and-burn their spending. Financial guru Dave Ramsey has what he calls a *rice and beans* meal plan: when you are in deep debt, you eat "beans and rice, rice and beans," to reduce spending in an easy to control area of your life while you work to eliminate your debt. Rice and beans are certainly cheap but can get old fast. I propose ramen as an addition to this mantra. It is a delicious and cheap staple that, as you will learn, can help you save some serious money in your eating budget of a short time frame.

The Cost of Eating

The average cost of eating out for one individual (one meal) in the United States is $12.75.[1] The average American eats an average of 4.2 meals out (broadly covering all commercially prepared meals) each week. Over the course of a year, that is a total of $2,784.60 a year spent eating out—and that doesn't even include the cost of the meals eaten at home for the other 16.8 meals of the week! That cost brings the total closer to $6,235.32.

Let's take this calculation and move the meals to the home. The average cost of a home-cooked meal per person is $3.95. This can include meals prepared totally from scratch as well as frozen and pre-prepared meals. If you assume this is the cost of each meal of the day (perhaps accurate for breakfast, but a rather generous estimate for dinner costs) and

---

[1] A thanks to The Simple Dollar for providing the statistics:
https://www.thesimpledollar.com/dont-eat-out-as-often-188365/

extrapolate it to each of the 21 meals of the week, this amount still totals $4,313.40.

It is in response to these costs that many people are turning to meal planning. Many businesses and websites sell weekly and monthly meal plans to help people reduce the cost of their meals down to $3.00, $2.00, or even less per person. Food is an effective place for someone to cut their budget once they've eliminated their extra expenses. If someone has cut their discretionary spending and still finds themselves scraping by to cover the essentials, it makes sense to look at their eating habits.

But What if this Isn't Enough?

Sometimes people go through periods in their lives where they need to use their diet to supplement their budget. Anyone who has gone through college has probably personally experienced a period of eating butter spaghetti, PB&Js, or banana toast (or certainly knew someone who did). Sometimes this happens outside of school as well, when someone has to watch what they eat to ensure the lights stay on.

The Origins of the Ramen Budget

Other times, people try to engage in extreme money-saving measures for short times to meet financial goals. This is where I came in. I have been privileged enough in my family background and personal finances to not have to worry about choosing between electricity and food. There have been times though where I've had to be extremely critical about my budget to accomplish my goals and adhere to my budget. Several years ago, I spent a year studying and working in Norway. Annual reports regularly find Norway to be in the top five most expensive countries to live in the world. Food prices in are 60% higher than the average grocery price in Europe.

For Norwegians, the high costs are reasonable. Many of the things that comprise a large part of a household's budget in the United States (like health care, medicine, school, college, and retirement pensions) are covered through Norway's comprehensive welfare system, opening up a greater portion of the household budget to spending on food and entertainment. But for a foreign student living on savings and a club bouncer's income (mostly paid in beer and cider), those food costs could add up fast.

To accomplish the things I wanted to do during this year—mostly centered on experiences—I had to prioritize my spending. I ended up creating a meal plan that became the origins of the Ramen Budget. By utilizing cheap ingredients and repeated meals, I was able to save money that helped me travel around Norway during my time there. I stayed in budget hostels and did a *lot* of walking (my calves looked great by the end), but I fulfilled my experiential goals.

Later, in graduate school, I used this meal plan to save money to help cover the fees associated with attending conferences in my discipline. My university offered travel grants, but students could only apply for them one every two or three years, depending on the grant. For the first time in my life, I had a regular paycheck from teaching at my campus's writing center. Sure, it was only $15,000 a year (and tuition waived), but it was the most I had ever made in my life! This thrill quickly wore out as I realized how fast food costs added up. At that time, suggestions that I eat out less were of not help whatsoever—I wasn't doing that in the first place! Instead, I had to get critical about what I was making at home. As a bit of creative spirit, I tried to get as fancy as I could using the same repeated ingredients.

The only downside of using these repeated ingredients was that they tended to be shelf-stable and carb-heavy. Therefore, I started to experiment more with incorporating vegetables (but not too many! Fresh veggies were hard on the wallet) and other healthy ingredients. And BOOM—I wrote the recipes down and gave them a title: The Ramen Budget Cookbook.

It was during my final year of graduate school that my ramen budget was put to the test. I had do some fieldwork that would require me to take a long road trip and alternative camp and stay in motels for two weeks. The kicker: I had less than 90 days to get the money for everything. As someone who was both a millennial and graduate student, I had prided myself on never carrying a credit card balance from one month to the next (paid on the 16th every time, baby!) and didn't want to start then. So I put myself on a two-month ramen budget diet. Sure enough, spending less than a dollar per meal added up. I was able to do my fieldwork without going into debt—no matter how short—and was able to continue my saving eating habits during the fieldwork as well!

It's been a couple years and several evolutions, but *The Ramen Budget* is now put together. I've gone beyond recipes, providing comprehensive cost breakdowns for the recipes. I have tried to be accurate, but erred on the side of generosity of the prices—it's more fun to see that the prices of ingredients in your area are cheaper than anticipated… plus I live in an expensive city!

I'm excited to share this knowledge with you, and hope that you can use it to quickly re-allocate your funds during times of exceptional need, exceptional opportunity, or even exceptional budget or diet experimentation!

On the Limits of Individual Actions: A Disclaimer

Let me be frank: there is something intrinsically troubling about a system where students, adults—anyone—should go hungry or have to restrict their diet in order to cover their bills or take care of necessary payments. That being said, there are times where individuals need to temporarily engage in serious money-saving practices in order to accomplish their financial needs or goals.

That's where the idea for this book came in. If people are going to find extra money and flexibility in their food budget, then at the very least they should have resources to ensure they have diversity in their diets, a guide to making warm and comforting meals, and enough vegetables and other healthy ingredients to make sure they are not depriving themselves of key vitamins or nutrients.

The recipes in this book seek to incorporate a healthy amount of vegetables in each meal. That being said, ramen is inherently high in salt and carbohydrates. Whether you are eating the recipes in this book out of necessity, fun, or an intensive-money saving window, this 'meal plan, if you will, is meant to be short term. If you feel unwell or notice that a ramen-heavy diet is not agreeing with you, stop, or look into spacing out your ramen meals. I personally had a period of two months of ramen-based eating, and that was my cap. If I had to carry things further, I would have cut down my ramen-based meals to once a day. Know your body and adjust what you eat as needed.

The Math of The Ramen Budget

The savings you experience will depend on how many meals you eat from this book each day, as well as how long you do the ramen budget meal plan. The following plans show potential averages that can be saved based on how dominant ramen-based meals are in your diet and how long you fulfill the budget

The following calculations are based on the average at-home meal cost of $3.95 and the average ramen budget meal price of $1.17

		Ramen Meals Per Day		
		1 Meal	2 Meals	3 Meals
Length of Ramen Budget Diet	1 week (7 days)	$19.46	$38.92	$58.38
	3 weeks (21 days)	$58.38	$116.96	$175.14
	1 month (31 days)	$86.18	$172.36	$258.54
	2 months (61 days)	$169.58	$339.16	$508.74
	3 months (92 days)	$255.76	$511.52	$767.28

Recently Suze Orman stirred up a bit of a controversy when she tweeted about the financial cost of "the latte factor" (a purchase-power thought exercise that has been around since the late 1980s. Basically, she claimed that with the money that an individual uses to buy a daily coffee every day over the course of their adult life, people loose out on over a million dollars that could have been built up in their retirement savings.

The sources of the controversy stemmed from several different areas. Some people criticized the math used to calculate the conversion of coffee-costs to retirement bucks (Orman rounded up to $3.00 per coffee, estimated several decades of potential growth with a generous growth estimate of 11% annually). Others criticized the advice for denying people of life's little joys that make the day more bearable.

While the previous calculations come a little close to Orman's latte factor calculations, a couple key things make the ramen budget a little more realistic. First, the savings are examined in the short-term. Interest isn't really accumulating at the three-month mark, and the budget is supposed to help re-allocate money that would otherwise be spent in this smaller time frame. Second, if you're already looking into re-allocating your money and food purchases, you're probably already okay with temporarily giving up some of food-related 'little joys'. Well, that, or you just really love ramen!

Price Breakdown

The cost of each recipe is included in its description. The costs fall within four ranges, based on the total price of all ingredients:

$: Under $0.75

$$: $0.76-1.30

$$$: $1.31-$1.90

$$$$: $1.91 and higher

As you will see, this is no Michelin scale. Four dollar signs does not mean costly, except in relation to other recipes in this book. All but two recipes of this book fall under $2.00

Ingredients and Costs

Using the average prices for standard grocery items in the United States for February 2019[2], I provide a guide for all the ingredients used in this cookbook. The prices here are shown for full-size items (even though you'll use one egg in the "Ramen Omelet" recipe, the list gives the price of a full dozen.

Many of the items you'll find in this list are common kitchen staples (soy sauce, potatoes, etc), and other are items you can get from single-serving packets at fast food chains (red pepper flakes, salt and pepper packets). These items are included to help give a picture of the total cost for buying all required ingredients, even the ones that are only used for one or two recipes. The idea is to show the low start-up cost for stocking your kitchen for the Ramen Budget.

Even here, you'll find that many of the ingredients can be substituted. Instead of getting both ground beef and ground chicken, you can use ground chicken for all recipes requiring ground meat. Ground and whole chicken are provided as two separate purchases; however, because of the different ways each ingredient is used.

Each recipe will provide a further breakdown of the ingredient cost according to the amount used.

Ingredients and Cost Breakdown

Ramen, 1 packet: $0.25[3]

Meat
Bacon, ½ lb: $4.80
Ground Beef, ½ lb: $2.80
Ground chicken, ½ lb $1.93
Ham, canned: $1.25

---

[2] https://www.globalprice.info/en/?p=usa/food-prices-in-usa
[3] The price of ramen can vary from $0.11 to $.50 depending on where you buy it, whether it is on sale or you have coupons, and which brand you buy. This book uses an average based on states and store prices.

Pork on the bone, ½ lb: $3.70
Whole Chicken, ½ lb: $1.30

Dairy and Eggs
Eggs, one dozen large grade AA eggs: $1.87
Margarine (not butter), 45 oz: $3.76
Milk ½ gallon $1.67
Parmesan: $2.83
Romano Cheese: $4.48
Shredded Cheese, ½ lb: $2.70

Furits and Vegetables
Avocado $1.10
Baby spinach $3.99
Banana: $0.49
Bell Pepper: $.89
Broccoli, ½ lb: $1.60
Cabbage: $1.89
Carrot 1 lb: $0.88
Celery: $1.98
Celery: $1.98
Cream of corn: $0.75
Cucumber: $0.68
Frozen mixed veggies, 12 oz: $1.00
Frozen peas: $1.00
Garlic chopped, 1 head: $0.48
Green onion bunch: $0.98
Iceberg lettuce: $1.48
Onion: $0.62
Pineapple, Canned: $0.98
Potatoes, ½ lb: $0.70
Strawberries, 1 lb: $2.99
Tomato paste, 1 can: $0.93
Tomatoes, ½ lb: $1.40
Zucchini: $0.79

Herbs and Seasonings
Cayenne: $3.24
Cilantro leaves: $0.48
Curry powder: $2.97

Furikake: $3.19
Garlic powder, 69 oz: $5.98
Ginger, ground: $3.96
Paprika: $3.97
Parsley 1 oz: $3.06
Pepper 6 oz: $4.08
Red pepper flakes: $2.20
Salt, 26 oz: $3.48

Oil, Sauces, and Condiments
Apple Cider Vinegar, 1 gal: $2.59
Balsamic Vinegar: $4.94
Chicken broth, 32 oz: $1.29
Cinnamon, 1.75 oz: $3.63
Coconut milk, can: $0.89
Cornstarch: $1.79
Fish Sauce: $2.42
Hoisin sauce: $4.12
Ketchup: $0.89
Lemon juice: $0.88
Lime juice, 32 oz: $2.46
Mirin: $4.25
Olive oil, 17 oz: $8.97
Red curry paste: $2.41
Sesame oil: $2.72
Siracha, 16 oz: $5.39
Soy sauce: $1.99
Sugar, 2 lb: $2.24
Vanilla extract: $3.11
Vegetable oil, 1 gal: $4.86
Worcestershire sauce: $3.10

Other
Almonds, 14 oz: $4.97
Bread, 1 loaf: $1.38
Chili, can: $0.89
Chocolate bar: $0.89
Flour, 5 lb: $2.26
Flour tortilla, 20 count: $2.18

Honey: $2.98
Marshmallows, 1 bag: $1.59
Mushrooms, 12 oz: $2.08
Navy beans, 1 can: $0.65
Peanuts: $5.34
Peanut Butter, 40 oz: $2.47
Seaweed sheets: $1.00
Sugar, 1 lb: $1.22
Vegetable bouillon: $4.15
Whipped Cream, $1.88
White Chocolate Chips: $2.98

Total Cost of Ingredients: $163.43

Wow! Sans ramen, *all* the ingredients that will get you through the recipes of this book costs less than $165! Even more impressive is the realization that many of these ingredients are things that are common in pantries or fridges. Even more ingredients will have amounts left over after when you're done with the budget diet! For example, you probably won't be using a whole gallon of vegetable oil in these recipes, or a 69oz container of garlic powder! These sizes are chosen because of their availability and to help calculate the average cost of the ingredients used in recipes.

Cutting Costs Further on Ingredients

To help balance out large or more expensive ingredients, the following ingredients are easy to find for free at restaurants, bulk stores, or elsewhere:

Butter/Margarine packets
Parmesan cheese packets
Crushed red pepper packets
Salt packets
Pepper packets
Ketchup packets
Honey packets

Vinegar packets
Peanut butter packs

The Recipes

Breakfast

Scrambled eggs

$$

$0.82

A classic, made more hearty with the addition of some filling carb noodles.

1 package ramen noodles (any flavor) $0.25
1 Tbsp vegetable oil $0.02
2 eggs $0.32
1 tsp dried parsley $0.02
¼ onion $0.20
1 tsp water
A pinch of salt and pepper $0.01

Directions

Bring a pot of water to a boil. Add the ramen noodles and a dash of salt and cook for 3 minutes.

While the noodles cook, finely chop up the onion.

Once the noodles have cooked, drain the water. Add the seasoning packet and dried parsley to the noodles and stir to combine.

Coat the bottom of a small pan with oil and bring to medium heat. Add the chopped onion and cook until the onion is translucent. Stir frequently to prevent the onion from burning.

Add the ramen noodles and cook for one more minute.

In a separate bowl, whisk the eggs, water, and salt together. Pour the egg mixture over the noodles and onion.

Cook the eggs, until cooked through.

Omelet

$

$0.70

Onion and ramen noodles fill both the omelet folds and one's stomach.

1 package ramen noodles $0.25
2 eggs $0.32
1 tsp vegetable oil $0.01
1 tsp garlic powder $0.04
1 green onion $0.08

Directions

Wisk the eggs and garlic powder in a bowl, adding the ramen seasoning to taste. Thinly slice the green onion.

Add water to a pot and add the noodles. Once the noodles are cooked, drain them and rinse to prevent them from cooking further. Place on a towel to absorb excess water.

As the noodles drain, heat a pan over medium heat and add the vegetable oil. Once hot, add the ramen noodles and fry until they begin to crisp.

Add the eggs, making sure to coat the bottom of the pan. Top with the sliced green onion.

Cook the omelet for two minutes, then flip the mix. Cook the second side for another two minutes.

Fold the omelet before serving.

Ramen Crusted French Toast

$$

$1.24

Ramen adds a perfect crunch while adding some intrigue to an otherwise classic breakfast dish.

1 package ramen $0.25
3 eggs $0.48
¼ cup milk $0.03
4 slices bread (preferably stale) $0.24
2 Tbsp margarine, divided $0.09
1 tbsp sugar $0.01
1 tsp ground cinnamon $0.06
1 teaspoon vanilla extract $0.07
pinch salt $0.01

Directions

Put the noodles in a baggie and crush into fine crumbs with a rolling pin or other heavy instrument.

In a pan, melt 1 Tbsp of margarine. Add the sugar and cinnamon and stir until the sugar has melted. Crumble the ramen noodles into the pan and cook for three minutes until the noodle crumbles are covered in the sugar-spice mixture. Remove from the heat and let cool, transferring into a shallow bowl.

In a bowl, mix the eggs, milk, vanilla, and salt.

In the pan, add the second Tbsp of margarine and bring to medium heat. Dip and coat the first slice of bread into the egg batter, then the sugar-spice mixture. Lay on the hot pan and cook about three minutes on the first side. When the slice is golden brown, flip it and cook an additional two minutes, until the second side is also golden brown.

Fry the remaining slices of bread.

Breakfast Scramble

$$$$

$1.94

Bacon makes this dish luscious. A little fat brings out the savory in the ramen seasoning.

2 packages of ramen $0.50
2 slices bacon $0.60
2 eggs $0.32
½ cup shredded cheese $0.23
2 green onions $0.16
1 tsp siracha $0.05
1 tsp extra-virgin olive oil $0.04
½ tsp pepper $0.01

Directions

Chop the bacon into ½-inch slices. In a bowl, beat the eggs until well-incorporated. Add the cheese and set aside.

Thinly slice the green onions.

Boil the ramen noodles according to package instructions. Once cooked, drain and reserve ¼ cup of cooking water. Toss the noodles with oil.

Cover the bottom of a pan with oil and bring to medium-high heat. Cook the bacon until crisp. Use reserved cooking water to loosen any bacon fat or pieces from the pan.

Add the noodles to the bacon and cover them with the oil and bacon. Add the eggs, green onions, pepper, and siracha.

Let the eggs cook until solid on the bottom. Stir the mix and cook about 5 minutes until the eggs are cooked through and the cheese is soft.

Breakfast Veggie

$$

$1.13

Vegetables make the addition of ramen a little healthier. No need to snack before lunch when having this dish.

1 package ramen noodles $0.25
1 Tbsp olive oil $0.09
1 Tbsp lemon juice $0.04
½ tsp salt $0.01
¼ tsp pepper $0.04
½ avocado $0.65
1 tsp furikake $0.05

Directions

Cook the ramen noodles according to the package directions. Once cooked, strain and rinse in cold water to prevent further cooking.

Toss the noodles with olive oil, lemon juice, salt, pepper, and furikake and place on a plate.

Slice the avocado into ¼ inch slices and place on top of the ramen noodles.

Breakfast Burrito

$$$

$1.56

Ramen noodles replace rice or potatoes to stretch the burrito a little further. Go crazy on the siracha to make it more spicy!

2 cups water
1 package ramen noodles *$0.25*
1 egg *$0.16*
¼ cup shredded cheese *$0.11*
1 Tbsp siracha *$0.08*
1 tortilla *$0.10*

Directions

Cook the ramen noodles according to package directions.

Beat the egg in a bowl. Add the seasoning packet and cheese.

Add the egg mixture to a pan over medium-high heat. Cook until the eggs start to firm, then add the noodles. Cook for four minutes until cooked through and remove from heat.

Lay the ramen-egg mixture on the tortilla and pour on the hot sauce.

Wrap the filling in the tortilla.

Ramen Frittata

$$$

$1.56

This recipe takes a little longer than a scramble, but the results are well worth it!

2 cups water
1 package ramen noodles $0.25
3 eggs $0.48
¼ potato $0.15
pinch of salt $0.01
pinch of pepper $0.01
1 tsp vegetable oil $0.01

Directions

Cook the ramen noodles until al dente.

Chop the potato into small cubes

Beat the eggs in a bowl. Add the salt, pepper, ramen seasoning,

Fry the potato in vegetable oil in a small pan over medium-high heat.

Once the potato is soft and pierceable with a fork, add the ramen noodles and eggs.

Place a plate over the top of the pan. Reduce the heat to medium-low and cook for 5 minutes.

Carefully use a spatula to flip the frittata. Cook an additional 3 minutes on the other side.

Bacon and Egg Ramen

$$$$

$2.00

Bacon and spinach make this breakfast dish decadent, especially with chicken broth.

2 Tbsp oil $0.04
2 green onions $0.16
3 cloves garlic, minced $0.06
1 ½ cup chicken broth $0.30
2 tablespoons soy sauce $0.03
1 package ramen $0.25
1 cup baby spinach $0.40
1 egg $0.16
2 strips bacon $0.60

Directions

Mince the garlic and slice the green onions.

Soft boil the egg in a small pot (about 5-6 minutes). Remove from the heat and submerge in cold water. Once the egg is cool to the touch, peel it and set aside.

Slice the bacon into ½ inch slices. Cook in a lightly oiled pot with the garlic.

Add the chicken broth, soy sauce, and one cup of water to the bacon pot and bring to a boil, stirring occasionally to get any brown bits stuck to the bottom of the pot.

Add the ramen noodles and cook for three minutes.

Turn off heat. Slice the egg in half

Add the spinach and soft boiled egg halves. Garnish with the green onions.

Soup-Based Dishes

Pork Noodle Soup

$$$

$1.53

All the vegetables combine to create a smooth and hearty broth.

3 stalks celery $0.20
½ onion $0.31
1 Tbsp vegetable oil $0.03
2 cloves garlic $0.04
2 cups water
1/8 head cabbage $0.21
1 Tbsp dried parsley $0.03
Dash cayenne pepper $0.01
1 package ramen $0.25
½ cup sliced pork $0.45

Directions

Chop the celery, onion, cabbage, and mince the garlic.

Cook the pork in 1 tsp vegetable oil in a pot over high heat until crisp and cooked through

Sautee the celery, onion, and garlic in the same pot, adding the remaining oil. Add the water, cabbage, parsley, and cayenne. Bring to a boil.

Once at a boil, add the noodles and seasoning and boil for one minute. Reduce the heat and simmer for two minutes before serving.

Chicken and Noodle Tomato Soup

$$

$0.92

Noodles float suspended in this savory tomato broth. Fresh or frozen vegetables can be used in the recipe.

1/3 cup chicken, sliced $0.18
1 tsp vegetable oil $0.01
2 tsp vegetable bouillon $0.23
1 package noodles $0.25
1 tsp sugar $0.01
½ teaspoon pepper $0.01
¼ teaspoon salt $0.01
1 Tbsp tomato paste $0.06
1 ½ cup water
½ cup frozen mixed vegetables $0.16

Directions

In a pan, cook the chicken in vegetable oil until cooked through. Stir in the tomato paste, ramen seasoning, sugar, pepper, and salt. Cook for one minute.

Add the water, vegetable bouillon, and frozen vegetables. Bring to a boil and cook one minute. Reduce the heat to simmer and cook for five minutes.

Add the noodles and cook for three minutes, until noodles break apart and are tender.

Red Curry Carrot Soup

$$$$

$2.48

This soup is a bit of a splurge, but is well worth it. The carrots and coconut milk combine will with the red curry. Combining ingredients to make larger batches can also cut costs.

1 package ramen $0.25
3 garlic cloves $0.06
¼ onion $0.16
1 Tbsp vegetable oil $0.04
½ cup coconut milk $0.20
2 tsp red curry paste $0.13
1 tsp curry powder $0.08
½ cup ground beef $0.32
½ tsp parsley $0.02
½ tsp basil $0.02
¼ tsp pepper $0.01
¼ tsp salt $0.01
2 cups chicken broth $0.35
½ zucchini $0.37
½ carrot $0.03
¼ cup shredded cabbage $0.07
1 tsp soy sauce $0.02

Mince the garlic and chop the zucchini, onion, carrot, and cabbage.

Cook the ramen noodles according to package directions (discarding the ramen seasoning). Remove from the water once cooked.

Mix the ground beef with parsley, basil, pepper and salt. Form the meat into small balls. Fry over medium-high heat in a pan until fully cooked through. Remove the meatballs from the pan and add more vegetable oil to the pan.

Cook the garlic for one minutes. Add half the coconut milk, then the curry paste and curry powder.

Cook for five minutes, stirring occasionally. Add the meatballs, chicken broth, zucchini, onion, carrot, cabbage, soy sauce and remaining coconut milk.

Bring the mix to a boil then reduce hear.

Simmer until the carrot is soft. Add the noodles to the soup and serve warm.

Ham Ramen Navy Beans

$$$

$1.52

This soup is reminiscent of farm classics. Navy beans take in the flavor of the ham, egg, and chicken broth while also delivering protein.

1 cup navy beans $0.48
1/3 cup ham $0.35
1 Tbsp vegetable oil $0.04
2 cloves garlic $0.04
1 egg $0.16
1 green onion $0.08
1 sheet seaweed $0.10
¼ tsp salt $0.01
1 cup chicken broth $0.20
1 cup water
2 tsp mirin $0.04
1 tsp sugar $0.01
½ tsp ginger $0.01

Directions

Heat vegetable oil in a pot over medium-high heat. Chop the ham into ¼ inch cubes and add to the oil. Sautee until the sides begin to brown and become aromatic.

Add the garlic, green onion, mirin, sugar, and ginger. Let cook for one minute, being careful to not let the mix burn.

Meanwhile, soft boil an egg in a small pot.

Add the navy beans to the ham mixture, cooking for one minute.

Add the chicken broth and water and bring to a boil. Add the ramen noodles and cook for three minutes until soft.

Top with the soft boiled egg and crumbled seaweed sheet.

Potato Cheese Soup

$$

$0.87

Hoisin sauce adds an unexpected punch to an otherwise straightforward potato soup with cheese.

1 package ramen $0.25
½ potato $0.15
1 Tbsp vegetable oil $0.04
1/8 cup shredded cheese $0.05
½ onion $0.32
1 tsp hoisin sauce $0.04
Pinch salt $0.01
Pinch pepper $0.01

Directions

Slice the onion.

Slice the potato into long strips like French fries. Lightly salt and pepper the potato.

Heat the vegetable oil over medium-high heat in a pan. Add the potatoes and fry until soft and piercable with a fork. Once cooked, remove the potatoes from the heat.

Add more vegetable oil to the pan and add the sliced onion with a pinch of salt. Cook the onions until the are caramelized, about 20 minutes. Stir frequently to avoid burning. The onions will be a light brown when ready.

Cook the ramen noodles according to package directions, adding the seasoning and hoisin sauce. Place in a bowl and top with the cooked potatoes, cheese (it should melt quickly), and caramelized onions.

Ramen Corn Chowder

$$$

$1.40

Using canned corn instead of fresh or frozen means this dish can be pulled together at any time. Avoid adding salt or too much ramen seasoning to keep it from getting too salty.

½ can creamed corn *$0.37*
1 package ramen noodles *$0.25*
2 tsp vegetable oil *$0.02*
2 strips bacon *$0.60*
1 cup water
2 green onions *$0.16*

Directions

Add the can of creamed corn and water to a pot and bring to medium-high heat.

Slice the bacon into thin strips. In a separate pan, cook the bacon in vegetable oil and fry until crisp. Add the green onions and cook an additional minute.

Add the bacon, green onion, and seasoning packet to the corn chowder. Add the noodles and cook until soft, about 4 minutes.

Broccoli Soup

$

$0.57

This straightforward soup still takes in fresh and green ingredients while adding a classic ingredient: cheese.

2 cups water
½ cup broccoli $0.20
1 package ramen noodles $0.25
1/4 teaspoon garlic powder $0.01
¼ cup shredded cheese $0.11

Directions

Slice the broccoli

In a large saucepan, bring water to a boil. Add the broccoli and boil for three minutes. Crumble the ramen noodles and cheese and add them to the boiling water. Cook for three minutes.

Add the seasoning packet and garlic powder to the soup. Stir until the cheese is melted and well-incorporated.

Hot Noodle Dishes

Sesame Chicken Noodle

$$$

$1.44

Sesame oil imparts a more complex flavor than straightforward olive or vegetable oil. This dish is excellent warm, room temperature, or even cool.

1 tsp sesame oil $0.07
½ cup chicken $0.22
½ cup zucchini $0.37
1 carrot $0.06
¼ cup frozen peas $0.16
½ tsp garlic powder $0.02
1 package ramen noodles $0.25
1 cup water
½ cup chicken broth $0.09
2 teaspoons soy sauce $0.04
2 green onions $0.16

Directions

Julienne the carrots, chop the zucchini, and slice the green onions.

In a pan, cook the chicken, zucchini, carrot, and frozen peas over sesame oil until the chicken is cooked through, about six minutes.

Add the garlic powder and the ramen seasoning. Cook for 2 more minutes.

Add the water, chicken broth, soy sauce, and noodles. Bring to a boil and cook until the noodles are tender, about 3 minutes.

Serve topped with green onions.

Beef and Mushroom Sesame Noodles

$$

$1.01

Mushrooms may add a little more of a cost to the recipe, but they stretch the beef and soak up the flavors of the spices, sesame oil, and ground beef.

1 package ramen $0.25
1 tsp vegetable oil $0.01
¼ cup ground beef $0.16
¼ cup mushrooms $0.40
2 tsp margarine $0.04
Pinch salt $0.01
Pinch pepper $0.01
1 cup water
¼ cup cilantro leaves $0.06
1 tsp sesame oil $0.07

Directions

Slice the mushrooms. Sautee the mushrooms in the margarine over medium-high heat. Season with the salt and pepper. Once the mushrooms begin to turn soft, add the ground beef.

Cook until the beef is brown throughout, about 4 minutes. Add the ramen seasoning and sesame oil.

Add the water and ramen noodles. Bring to a boil and cook the noodles for 3 minutes. Remove from heat, serve, and top with torn cilantro leaves.

Break noodles into small pieces.

In a pan over medium heat, cook the beef in oil until brown throughout, about 5 minutes. Add the mushrooms, salt, pepper, and ramen seasoning. Cook an additional 5 minutes until the mushrooms are tender.

Add the broken noodles and water. Bring the heat to high and boil for 3 minutes until the noodles come apart.

Remove from the heat and stir in the cilantro and sesame oil. Serve warm.

Stir Fry Pork

$$

$1.29

At serving, the vegetables should be slightly crisp and coated with a slightly thickened sauce.

2 Tbsp soy sauce $0.03
2 tsp tomato paste $0.04
½ tsp Worcestershire sauce $0.03
½ tsp sugar $0.01
½ tsp red pepper flakes $0.03
2 Tbsp vegetable oil $0.08
½ cup pork chop, cut into cubes $0.42
Pinch salt $0.01
Pinch pepper $0.01
½ cup broccoli, chopped $0.20
½ cup cabbage, shredded $0.14
2 garlic cloves, minced $0.04
1 package ramen $0.25

Directions

Wisk together the soy sauce, tomato paste, Worcestershire sauce, sugar, and red pepper flakes.

Heat the vegetable oil in a pan over medium-high heat. Add the pork. Season with salt and pepper and fry for 4 minutes, until cooked through.

Add the Add the broccoli, cabbage and sauce mix. Fry 3 minutes, until the cabbage has wilted.

Cook the ramen noodles according to directions in a separate pot.

Drain the noodles and add to the pork mixture. Serve warm.

Chicken Lo Mein

$$$

$1.48

The vegetables in this lo mein, while holding different flavor profiles, have similar firmness and textures once cooked.

1 package ramen $0.25
2 Tbsp vegetable oil $0.08
½ cup chopped chicken $0.22
1 carrot $0.06
½ onion $0.32
1 stalk celery $0.06
½ tsp garlic powder $0.02
1 ½ cups water
1 cup shredded cabbage $0.28
¼ cup frozen peas $0.16
2 Tbsp soy sauce $0.03

Directions

Thinly slice the carrots, onion, and celery.

Heat the vegetable oil over medium-high in a pan. Once hot, add the chopped chicken and cook for two minutes until there is no pink left.

Add the carrots, celery, onion, cabbage, peas, soy sauce and garlic powder. Cook for 5 minutes, until everything is soft.

In a separate pot, cook the ramen noodles according to package instructions. Once cooked, drain and add to the chicken and vegetables. Serve warm.

Spinach Ramen

$$

$0.90

Fresh spinach takes the place of more hearty vegetables of other dishes to create a light, manageable dish that can be thrown together in a hurry.

1 package ramen $0.25
1 cup baby spinach $0.40
1 Tbsp olive oil $0.08
2 tsp balsamic vinegar $0.05
½ tsp salt $0.01
½ tsp crushed red pepper $0.03
1 Tbsp parmesan $0.08

Directions

Prepare the ramen noodles according to the package instructions. 1 minute before the noodles are finished, add the baby spinach.

When the spinach is wilted, remove and drain the water. Add the olive oil, balsamic vinegar, salt, crushed red pepper, and parmesan.

Toss to incorporate all ingredients. Serve warm.

Italian Cheese and Pepper Pasta

$$

$0.81

An Italian classic is streamlined to work well with kitchen staples, including a simplified selection of cheeses.

1 package ramen $0.25
½ cup water
3 Tbsp margarine $0.12
1 Tbsp olive oil $0.11
¼ cup romano $0.08
¼ cup parmesan $0.24
½ tsp black pepper $0.01

Directions

Add the water, margarine, olive oil and black pepper to a pot and bring to a boil.

Add the cheese and turn the heat to simmer.

Add the ramen noodles (not including the seasoning) and stir frequently to keep the noodles and cheese from clumping.

Once the noodles are soft, about 3 minutes, plate the dish and serve.

Teriyaki Meatballs and Ramen

$$$

$1.88

Ground chicken makes excellent meatballs, though tvp or ground beef could be used as alternatives if you want to mix things up.

Meatballs
½ cup ground chicken $0.55
1 slice stale bread $0.06
¼ onion $0.16
1 tsp sesame oil $0.07
1 egg $0.16
1 tsp balsamic vinegar $0.03
½ tsp ginger $0.01
1 tsp garlic powder $0.01

Sauce
1 clove garlic $0.02
1 tsp ginger $0.01
2 tsp soy sauce $0.04
1 tsp honey $0.03
1 tsp hoisin sauce $0.04

1 package ramen $0.25
1 cup cabbage, shredded $0.28
2 green onions $0.16

Directions

Crumble the stale bread into breadcrumbs.

Mince the onion and slice the green onion into thin slices.

Combine all the meatball ingredients in a shallow bowl. Form into balls. Heat a pan with vegetable oil and fry the meatballs until cooked through.

Whisk together all of the ingredients for the sauce and add it to the meatballs. Cook for one minute then remove from the heat.

Boil 2 cups of water in a pot. Add the cabbage and noodles and cook for 3 minutes until the noodles and cabbage are soft. Drain all and put the noodles and cabbage into a bowl. Pour the sauce over the

When the meatballs are done, remove the baking sheet from the oven and set aside. Drop the noodles and cabbage into the boiling water, and cook for 3 minutes, until the noodles are soft. Drain, and place the cabbage and noodles in a large bowl. Top with the meatballs and sauce, then the green onions.

Pasta Salads

Strawberry Ramen Salad

$$$

$1.42

This is one of the few sweet salads in the recipe collection. Balsamic complements the natural tang of the strawberries while tying them to the firm noodles.

1 package ramen $0.25
¼ cup peanuts $0.30
2 tsp margarine $0.04
2 Tbsp sugar $0.02
2 tsp vegetable oil $0.02
2 tsp balsamic vinegar $0.05
2 tsp soy sauce $0.04
1 ½ cup lettuce $0.22
1 green onion $0.08
½ cup strawberries $0.40

Directions

Chop the peanuts and slice the strawberries and green onion.

Break the ramen noodles into small chunks, discarding packet.

Heat the margarine in a pan over medium heat and melt 1 tsp of sugar in the butter. Add the ramen noodles and peanuts and coat with the sugar mixture. Cook for two minutes, stirring frequently to prevent burning for five minutes.

Whisk the sugar, vinegar, soy sauce, and oil in a bowl.

Pour the dressing, walnut, ramen noodles, and strawberries over the lettuce.

Sesame Ramen Salad

$$$

$1.44

Fresh greenery and nuts add completing textures to the spiced noodles to create a recipe with layered crunch, smooth, and crisp feels.

1 package ramen $0.25
½ cup ground beef $0.32
1 tsp vegetable oil $0.01
½ tsp salt $0.01
1 tsp black pepper $0.01
½ tsp crushed red pepper $0.01
½ tsp paprika $0.01
½ tsp cayenne $0.01
2 green onions $0.16
½ cup cilantro $0.12
½ cup frozen peas $0.32
1 carrot $0.06
1/8 cup peanuts $0.15

Directions

Slice green onions. Julienne the carrot and chop the peanuts.

Blend the ground beef with the salt, black pepper, paprika, and cayenne.

Cover the noodles with boiling water and let sit and soften. Drain the noodles and let sit in a bowl.

Heat the vegetable oil over medium heat. Add the beef and frozen peas and cook until brown throughout, stirring frequently to make sure the ground beef does not clump.

Mix the ground beef, noodles, carrots, peanuts, cilantro, and green onion in a bowl.

Chicken Noodle Salad

$$$

$1.65

Take the soup out of chicken noodle, and you're left with a filling, cabbage-and chicken-heavy pasta salad!

3 Tbsp balsamic vinegar *$0.11*
2 Tbsp vegetable oil *$0.08*
3 Tbsp sugar *$0.03*
½ tsp pepper *$0.01*
1 package ramen *$0.25*
1 cup shredded cabbage *$0.28*
½ cup chicken, cooked *$0.22*
¼ cup sliced almonds *$0.38*
2 tsp sesame oil *$0.13*
2 green onions *$0.16*

Directions

Thinly slice the chicken into slices.

Toast the sliced almonds for 2 minutes.

Whisk vinegar, oils, sugar, pepper, and ramen seasoning.

Break the noodles into small pieces and mix with the cabbage and chicken. Coat with the dressing. Toss with the almonds and green onions.

Broccoli Noodle Salad

$$$

$1.34

Woody vegetables create good alternatives to the bulk of the noodles. The vinegar and sugar create a sweet-tangy glaze covering everything.

¾ cup shredded cabbage *$0.21*
½ cup broccoli *$0.20*
1 package ramen *$0.25*
2 green onions *$0.16*
¼ cup sliced almonds *$0.38*
3 Tbsp white sugar *$0.03*
3 Tbsp vegetable oil *$0.10*
2 Tbsp apple cider vinegar *$0.01*

Directions

Thinly chop the broccoli and green onions.

Break apart the ramen noodles.

In a large bowl, toss together the cabbage, noodles, almonds, and green onions.

Whisk together the sugar, oil, vinegar and ramen seasoning.

Pour the dressing over the salad and toss to coat all ingredients.

Cover and refrigerate the salad for an hour. Serve cool.

International Fusion

Hoisin Pork Tenderloin

$$

$1.00

This international fusion is perhaps the closest to its Asian-American fusion origins, getting closer to a Japanese dish with the inclusion of ramen noodles.

1 package ramen $0.25
3 Tbsp hoisin sauce $0.12
1 Tbsp soy sauce $0.01
2 tsp sugar $0.01
2 garlic cloves $0.04
½ tsp crushed red peppers $0.01
½ cup cubed pork $0.42
3 Tbsp water
1 Tbsp margarine $0.06
1 green onion $0.08

Directions

Mince the garlic cloves and slice the green onion.

In a pan over medium-high heat, add the pork and hoisin sauce. Cook until brown and crispy throughout. Add the water and bring the heat up until the sauce begins to boil.

Stir in the margarine, soy sauce, sugar, garlic, and crushed red peppers. Cook for an additional 4 minutes, until the sauce thickens, then remove from heat.

Cook the noodles according to the package directions, adding the ramen seasoning. Drain the noodles and serve into a bowl. Top with the pork hoisin and sliced green onion.

Ramen Latkes

$

$0.69

This dish has the combined benefit of lacking the nutritional benefit of potatoes and deviating from tradition! On the plus side, it retains the symbolic use of olive oil.

1 package ramen $0.25
2 green onions $0.16
3 Tbsp flour $0.01
1 egg $0.16
1 Tbsp olive oil $0.11

Directions

Slice the green onion. In a small bowl, beat the egg.

Cook the ramen according to package instructions. Drain. In a bowl, combine the ramen, green onions, flour, and egg.

Heat the olive oil over medium-high heat in a saucepan. Fry the ramen latke mix in the oil until brown on each side, about 2 minutes each side.

Pad Thai

$

$0.70

The trick to making this dish more authentic: using ketchup! While tamarind sauce is has been historically used, many modern pad thai recipes (even in Thailand) use ketchup now.

1 package ramen $0.25
1 egg $0.16
½ tsp soy sauce $0.01
1 tsp ketchup $0.01
1 tsp lime juice $0.03
3 Tbsp peanuts, crushed $0.08
2 green onions $0.16

Directions

Slice the green onions thinly.

Cook the noodles according to package instructions, not including the seasoning. Once the noodles are finished, remove from the water and drain.

In a separate bowl, crack and scramble an egg.

In the still-hot pan, drizzle in the egg. Cook scrambled until firm throughout.

In a large bowl, combine the noodles, scrambled egg, soy sauce, ketchup, lime juice, half of the ramen seasoning, crushed peanuts, and green onions

Peanut Thai Ramen

$

$0.46

Peanut butter adds a smooth, thick texture to ramen noodles made salty-spicy through siracha and soy sauce. The resulting dish is a deep, rich brown.

1 package ramen $0.25
½ tsp soy sauce $0.01
2 Tbsp peanut butter $0.04
1 Tbsp siracha $0.08
1 green onion $0.08

Directions

Prepare the ramen noodles according to package directions. Drain the water, reserving 3 Tbsp cup in the pot.

Add the soy sauce, peanut butter, and siracha to the reserve liquid. Reduce the heat to low and whisk all ingredients until smooth. Cook for 3 minutes.

Add the noodles and stir to coat. Serve with green onion as a garnish.

Ramen Katsu

$$

$1.19

This dish would fit perfectly in a bento box, topped with crisp, slightly acidic green onions.

½ cup pork, cut into strips $0.42
1 egg $0.16
1 package ramen noodles $0.25
1 cup chicken broth $0.17
2 tsp vegetable oil $0.02
1 green onion $0.08
3 clove garlic $0.06
½ carrot $0.03

Thinly slice the carrot so it will fry easily.

Break apart the noodles and reserve half. Pound half into fine crumbs.

Take the pork strips and cover them with the ramen seasoning. Dredge in the whisked egg, then dip in the ramen crumbs to coat them.

In a pan, heat the vegetable oil over high heat. Add the garlic and onion and fry for one minute. Add the carrot and potato. Once all ingredients are cooked, remove from the pan.

Now that the oil has been flavored with garlic, onion, and vegetables, fry the pork strips in the oil until brown and crispy, about 4 minutes on each side. Cut into the slices to make sure they are cooked through.

Once the pork strips are cooked, remove from the oil. Add the chicken broth and noodles. Bring to a boil and cook for 3 minutes.

To serve, add the ramen noodles to the bowl with as much broth as is preferred. Top with the friend vegetables, garlic, and onion, then the fried pork.

Pho Ramen

$

$0.62

This soup comes close to ramen in its common state—mirroring the salty, broth instant form. Added sauces and spices deepen the broth's flavor.

1 package ramen $0.25
¾ cup chicken broth $0.15
1 tsp line $0.03
1 tsp sugar $0.01
1 tsp fish sauce $0.03
½ tsp red pepper flakes $0.01
3 Tbsp cilantro leaves $0.03
¼ cup shredded cooked chicken $0.11

Directions

Cook the noodles in the chicken broth according to package directions. Once the noodles are cooked, add the lime, sugar, fish sauce, red pepper flakes, and chicken.

Top with cilantro leaves.

Tom Kha Goong

$

$0.73

Common Thai ingredients come together to create a filling, slightly spicy dish. The noodles soak up the broth, softening into smooth lengths.

1 package ramen noodles $0.25
½ cup coconut milk $0.20
1 tsp fish sauce $0.03
1 tsp sugar $0.01
1 Tbsp siracha $0.08
½ cup frozen vegetables $0.16

Directions

Cook the noodles according to directions, draining when finished.

Cook the frozen vegetables in the microwave until warm.

In a pot over medium heat, add the coconut milk, fish sauce, sugar, and siracha. Whisk and cook until heated through.

Add the vegetables and cook an additional two minutes. Add the noodles and stir to incorporate them with the sauce.

Serve warm.

Chimichanga

$

$0.60

After baking, the chimichangas have a crisp, enticing outer shell.

2 tortillas $0.20
½ cup cooked chicken $0.22
1 Tbsp and 1 tsp vegetable oil $0.05
2 garlic cloves, minced $0.04
2 tsp chili powder $0.03
1/8 cup shredded cheese $0.06

Directions

Preheat the oven to 350 degrees.

Heat a pan to medium-high heat and add 1 Tbsp vegetable oil, chicken, garlic, ramen noodle seasoning, and chili powder. Cook the chicken in the vegetable oil until no longer pink in the middle.

Cook the ramen noodles according to package directions.

Lay the two tortillas out. On each tortilla, add half the ramen noodles, chicken, and cheese. Roll the tortillas and place then seam side down on a baking sheet.

Drizzle the remaining vegetable oil over the tortillas. Bake for 7 minutes, until browned and crisp.

Noodle Pancakes

$$

$1.11

Rather than being sweet breakfast pancakes, this savory dish borrows from East Asian ingredients.

1 package ramen $0.25
½ zucchini $0.37
1 carrot $0.06
1 green onion $0.08
1 egg $0.16
4 Tbsp flour $0.01
1 tsp lime juice $0.03
2 Tbsp vegetable oil $0.08
2 Tbsp soy sauce $0.03
1 tsp sugar $0.01
1 Tbsp cider vinegar $0.01
1 tsp. red pepper flakes $0.02

Direction

Shred the zucchini and carrot. Slice the green onion.

Crumble the ramen noodles into large chunks and cook for 1 ½ minutes (do not add the seasoning packet). Drain the noodles.

In a bowl, mix the noodles, zucchini, carrot, green onion, flour, lime juice, and seasoning packet.

Beat the egg and add it to the bowl.

Add beaten eggs and mix well.

Heat a pan to medium-high heat. Add 2 Tbsp oil.

Use a large spoonful to transfer the noodle mixture to the pan. Ladle the mixture into a thick pancake shape. Fry for 3 minutes, then flip to the second side. Fry an additional 3 minutes. Cook the remaining batter.

Whisk together the soy sauce, vinegar, sugar, and red pepper flakes. Heat in a pan over medium heat until the mixture starts to thicken, about 4 minutes. Pour over the noodle pancakes.

Tropical Ramen

$$

$0.84

While less than authentic, this recipe certainly has ingredients borrowed from East Asian-American Pacific fusion dishes.

1/3 cup canned ham $0.35
2 tsp vegetable oil $0.02
¼ cup pineapple chunks $0.19
1 egg $0.16
2 tsp Worcestershire sauce $0.08
1 Tbsp soy sauce $0.02
2 Tbsp ketchup $0.02

Directions

Cook the ramen noodles according to package directions. Drain and set aside.

Heat the vegetable oil in a pan over high heat. Fry the spam in the oil until brown and crispy throughout.

Remove the spam from the pan and crack the egg into the same pan. Using the reserve oil and spam juice, fry the egg sunny side up (either over easy or hard, depending on your own preference).

Remove the egg from the pan and add the pineapple chunks, cooking until heated through.

Add the spam, egg, and pineapple to the noodles.

Whisk together the Worcestershire sauce, soy sauce, and ketchup in a bowl. Drizzle over the noodles.

Lettuce Wraps

$$$

$1.51

Noodles replace rice well in this delightful finger food.

1 package ramen noodles $0.25
1/3 cup shredded chicken, cooked $0.18
¼ bell pepper $0.22
¼ cucumber $0.17
½ carrot $0.03
2 green onions $0.16
2 Tbsp soy sauce $0.03
½ tsp chili powder $0.01
2 tsp sesame oil $0.13
2 cloves garlic $0.04
1 ½ tsp ginger $0.01
¼ iceberg lettuce $0.28

Directions

Chop the bell pepper, cucumber, and carrot and slice the green onion. Mince the garlic.

Bring water to boil in a pot. Crush the ramen and cook it with the seasonings until al dente, about 1 ½ minutes. Drain and rinse with cold water to prevent them from cooking further.

Mix the noodles, chicken, bell pepper, and green onions in a bowl.

Whisk together the sesame oil, garlic, ginger, and chili powder. Pour the blend into the bowl to stir and coat everything. Refrigerate the mixture as you prepare the lettuce.

Tear individual lettuce leave out and clean them. Lay the leaves flat on a preparation surface. Place a spoonful of topping on top of each lettuce leaf. Top the noodle mix with cucumber and carrot shreds.

Serve cool.

Fast Food Fusion

Ramen Tacos

$$

$0.97

Taco seasonings could replace chili powder, depending on whether one is a fan of cumin-heavy dishes.

2 tortillas $0.20
½ tsp chili power $0.01
½ tsp garlic powder $0.01
½ tsp red pepper flakes $0.01
¼ tsp paprika $0.01
¼ tsp cumin $0.01
¼ tsp salt $0.01
¼ tsp black pepper $0.01
1 package ramen $0.25
½ cup ground beef $0.32
2 tsp vegetable oil $0.08
¼ cup shredded lettuce $0.05

Directions

Heat vegetable oil in a pan over medium-high heat. Once hot, add the ground beef and all spices. Cook until the ground beef is almost completely brown.

Crush the ramen noodles into small chunks. Add the ramen noodles to the ground beef and cook until the noodles have softened slightly.

Divide the mixture between the two tortillas. Top with the lettuce. Wrap and enjoy.

Ramen Burger

$$

$1.26

This American-inspired dish is more carb-heavy than most international fusion dishes, but is a fun splurge.

2 packages ramen *$0.50*
¼ tsp pepper *$0.01*
½ cup ground beef *$0.32*
1 tsp soy sauce *$0.01*
4 Tbsp vegetable oil *$0.15*
2 Tbsp cheese *$0.03*
2 Tbsp ketchup *$0.03*
3 lettuce leaves *$0.05*
1 egg *$0.16*

Directions

Cook the ramen according to package directions (reserving the seasoning). Drain and set apart.

Beat the egg in a bowl and add the ramen seasoning and pepper. Stir the noodles into the eggs and ensure they are coated.

Divide the noodles into four portions.

Heat vegetable oil in a pan. Pour the first portion of ramen noodles and egg into a circular cookie mold or alternative circular form and fry the ramen/egg mixture until crisp, about 3 minutes. Flip the bun and fry an additional 3 minutes. Repeat for each noodle portion.

Add the ground beef and soy sauce in a bowl and stir to combine. Divide into two portions. Flatten each into a disk.

Fry the two burger disks in the pan until cooked through, about 5 minutes each side.

On the second side of the burger, sprinkle 1 Tbsp of cheese. Allow the cheese to soften and melt.

Arrange the burgers in the following order: ramen bun, lettuce, burger, ketchup, then top bun.

Sweet & Sour Ramen

$

$0.60

No one can deny the appeal of a simple, vividly red sweet-sour sauce!

¼ cup white sugar *$0.04*
3 Tbsp apple cider vinegar *$0.02*
1/8 cup water
2 Tbsp soy sauce *$0.03*
2 tsp ketchup *$0.02*
¾ tsp cornstarch *$0.02*
¼ bell pepper *$0.22*
1 package ramen *$0.25*

Chop the bell pepper into medium chunks.

Cook the ramen in water until it is al dente, about 2 minutes.

Remove the ramen from the heat and drain.

In a pot, whisk together the sugar, vinegar, water, soy sauce, ketchup, and cornstarch. Heat to medium and cook the sauce until it begins to thicken.

Pour the sweet and sour sauce over the ramen noodles and enjoy.

Cheesy Chili Ramen

$$

$0.76

This dish screams comfort food with meaty, bean-full chili and melted cheese on top.

¼ can chili *$0.22*
¼ onion, chopped *$0.16*
2 tsp vegetable oil *$0.08*
3 Tbsp shredded cheese *$0.05*
1 package ramen *$0.25*

Directions

Cook the ramen as directed on the package.

Drain the noodles once cooked.

In a pan, heat the oil over medium-high heat. Add the onion and cook until the onion is translucent, about 5 minutes.

Add the chili in the pan and cook until heated through. Top the noodles with the chili and the shredded cheese.

Ramen Poutine

$

$0.54

Ramen travels to northern North America. While perhaps sacrilegious to tamper with poutine's ingredients, this dish is a national favorite while using budget ingredients.

1 package ramen $0.25
1 cup chicken broth $0.17
2 tsp margarine $0.04
4 Tbsp flour $0.02
4 Tbsp shredded cheese $0.06

Melt the margarine in a pan over medium heat. Add the flour and whisk it in the margarine until the flour is browned and the ingredients are mixed.

Slowly add the chicken broth and stir until the mix creates a gravy. Stir occasionally over high heat until the gravy thickens, between 5 to 10 minutes.

Remove the gravy from the heat.

Heat the vegetable oil over medium heat. Break up the ramen into small chunks and fry in the oil until golden brown.

Pour the gravy over the ramen. Top with the shredded cheese.

Microwave the mix until the cheese bubbles, about 30 seconds.

Ramen Pizza

$

$0.49

While the ramen noodles seem like they will let through some tomato sauce, they will catch it and absorb it into a soft crust at the pizza cooks.

1 package ramen *$0.25*
3 Tbsp tomato sauce *$0.18*
3 Tbsp shredded cheese *$0.05*
½ tsp basil *$0.01*

Preheat the oven to 350 degrees.

Break the ramen package in half into two thin squares. Spoon tomato paste over each half and top with the shredded cheese.

Sprinkle basil on top of the cheese.

Bake the ramen pizza in the oven for 5 minutes until the cheese bubbles.

Ramen White Pizza

$$

$0.83

White sauce is never boring when Italian spices are added before getting the dairy broiled in the oven.

1 package ramen $0.25
1 tsp olive oil $0.03
2 cloves garlic $0.04
1 tsp red pepper flakes $0.01
½ tsp oregano $0.01
½ tsp basil $0.01
3 Tbsp parmesan $0.23
¼ cup milk $0.03
2 tsp margarine $0.02
2 Tbsp flour $0.01
1 egg $0.16
¼ tsp pepper $0.01

Directions

Preheat oven to 350 degrees.

Mince the garlic.

In a pan over medium heat, cook the olive oil, garlic, and red pepper flakes.

Divide the ramen noodles into two large thin squares. Place in an oven-safe pan.

In the pan, melt the margarine and add the flour. Stir the flour until browned and absorbed in the margarine. Add the milk little by little, stirring well to ensure the mix is well incorporated.

Add the basil, oregano, and pepper. Cook until the sauce begins to thicken.

Remove the sauce from the heat and pour over the ramen noodles. Top with the olive oil, garlic, and red pepper flakes.

Sprinkle the parmesan onto the top of the noodles.

Bake the white pizza for 10 minutes until the cheese begins to brown.

Desserts

Ramen Brownies

$$$

$1.64

Ramen is a good filling in these brownies, mirroring the role of nuts or chocolate chips.

8 ounces chocolate (chopping up a chocolate bar is cost-efficient) $0.40
½ cup margarine $0.20
3/4 cup flour $0.08
3 large eggs $0.48
1 cup sugar $0.16
1 tsp vanilla extract $0.07
1 package ramen $0.25

Directions

Preheat oven to 350 degrees.

Add the chocolate and butter to a microwave safe bowl. Microwave in increments of 10 seconds, stirring between each microwaving session. The mixture is done when smooth.

In another bowl, beat the eggs and sugar.

Add the vanilla and beat.

Add the chocolate mixture and beat.

Fold in the flour.

Break apart the ramen noodles into small chunks and add to the batter.

Pour the batter into a pan.

Bake for 18 minutes. Let cook before serving.

Ramen Krispies

$$$

$1.38

Ramen adds a fun crunch compared to smaller, flakier cereal, which usually features in this dessert.

3 packages ramen $0.75
1 ½ cup marshmallows $0.53
2 Tbsp margarine $0.09
¼ tsp salt $0.01

Directions

Discard the ramen seasoning.

Crush the ramen into small chunks.

Microwave the margarine in a microwave-safe bowl for 20 seconds, until melted. Pour the marshmallows in the bowl, stir to coat with margarine, then microwave in 30 second increments until the marshmallows puff up.

Mix the salt and ramen in the marshmallow puff until the ramen is completely coated. Pour into a firm-edged container and let cool to form.

Cut into squares to eat.

Strawberry Ramen Shortcake

$

$0.61

This fruit-based dessert has a lighter, more delicate sweetness than the chocolate-based recipes.

1 package ramen noodles $0.25
¼ cup strawberries $0.20
2 tsp honey $0.06
1 dash cinnamon $0.01
1 dash sugar $0.01
1/3 cup whipped cream $0.08

Directions

Cook ramen according to package directions, but discarding the seasoning.

Chill the noodles in the fridge. Add honey, cinnamon, and sugar.

Add a dollop of whipped cream and top with strawberries.

White Chocolate Ramen Bark

$$

$1.20

While white chocolate doesn't really have chocolate in it, this bark is nonetheless fantastic around the holidays.

1 package ramen $0.25
1 Tbsp and ½ tsp margarine $0.04
1 cup white chocolate chips $0.90
1 Tbsp milk $0.01

Directions

Use the ½ tsp of margarine and grease a cooking sheet.

Break the ramen into small chunks.

Place the white chocolate in a microwave-safe bowl and microwave at 30 second increments, stirring between. Continue until the chocolate is smooth. Add the margarine and milk and stir until well incorporated.

Pour the mix on the cooking sheet and sprinkle the ramen over the bark mixture.

Let cook, then break into chunks for eating.

Banana-Coconut Ramen Pudding

$$$

$1.79

Pudding and ramen are excellent mates, as this and the next recipe will demonstrate. Sweet and salty always pair well together!

1 package ramen $0.25
3 Tbsp margarine $0.11
2 eggs $0.32
½ cup sugar $0.08
¾ cup coconut milk $0.30
½ tsp vanilla extract $0.03
dash salt $0.01
½ tsp ground ginger $0.01
1 banana $0.49
1/8 cup almonds $0.19

Directions

Preheat the oven to 350 degrees.

Cook the noodles until al-dente. Disregard the ramen spice packet.

Drain the ramen noodles and toss with the margarine.

Whisk the eggs, sugar, coconut milk, vanilla, salt, and ginger in a bowl. Stir in the noodles and almonds in the mixture.

Slice the banana into thin slices and layer them on the bottom of a oven-safe pan.

Pour the pudding mixture over the banana.

In a small oven-safe pan, add one cup of water.

Bake the pudding in the oven alongside the water until the pudding has set, about 45 minutes.

Flan Ramen

$

$0.51

Flan from scratch has never been easier! Whisking the flan with the ramen noodles creates a surprisingly addictive dessert.

1 package ramen $0.25
¼ cup milk $0.03
1 egg $0.16
1 pinch salt $0.01
¼ cup sugar $0.04
1 dash vanilla extract $0.02

Directions

Preheat the oven to 325 degrees.

Whisk milk, egg, salt, sugar, and vanilla extract well. Pour into a bake-safe container. Place the bake-safe container in a larger baking pan half-full with water.

Bake until the custard sets, about half an hour.

Cook the ramen according to instructions. Drain.

Pour the flan over the ramen noodles and serve.

Snacks

Ramen Crunch Mix

$$$

$1.66

Crush mixes are always fantastic snacks. This salty, slightly spicy mix can use any oil to get the spices sticking to the nut and ramen chunks.

2 packages ramen $0.50
¼ cup peanuts $0.30
¼ cup almonds $0.38
1 cup cereal (any non-sweet favorite, such as cornflakes or cheerios) $0.30
2 Tbsp vegetable oil $0.08
1 tsp curry powder $0.08
½ tsp cayenne pepper $0.01
½ tsp salt $0.01

Directions

Preheat the oven to 350 degrees.

Break the ramen into small pieces.

Chop the peanuts and almonds into chunks.

In a bowl, toss all ingredients together until the ramen, peanuts, almonds, and cereal are all coated with oil and spices. Place on a baking pan.

Bake 7 minutes, then let cool before serving or putting into a container.

Sweet Ramen Crunch

$$

$1.24

Honey gets sweet seasonings to stick to the ramen, peanuts, and cereal, taking the place of oil.

2 packages ramen $0.50
¼ cup peanuts $0.30
1 cup cereal (any non-sweet favorite, such as cornflakes or cheerios) $0.30
2 Tbsp honey $0.12
½ tsp salt $0.01
½ tsp cinnamon $0.01

Directions

Break the ramen into small pieces.

Chop the peanuts into chunks.

In a bowl, toss all ingredients together until the ramen, peanuts, almonds, and cereal are all coated with honey and spices.

www.ingramcontent.com/pod-product-compliance
Lightning Source LLC
Chambersburg PA
CBHW031923170526
45157CB00008B/3030